My Little Basket of Gratitudes

Reflections of Life's Blessings,
Big and Small

By

NIRMALA ROOP SINGH

Edited by

CHRISTABEL SINGH

Clever Fox PUBLISHING
Chennai • Bangalore

CLEVER FOX PUBLISHING
Chennai, India

Published by CLEVER FOX PUBLISHING 2025

ISBN: 978-93-6707-974-4

Contents

Foreword

It is with profound honour and heartfelt admiration that I offer this foreword to Nirmala Roop Singh's deeply moving and spiritually enriching book. This remarkable work stands as a testament to the resilience of faith and the boundless grace of God, who walks with us through every season of life, especially during times of trial and uncertainty.

In these pages, Nirmala courageously shares her personal journey - a journey marked by challenges, setbacks, and moments of profound despair. Yet, through it all, she remained steadfast in her trust in the Lord. Her story is one of unwavering faith, a faith that was not merely a passive belief but an active force that guided her, comforted her, and ultimately led her through the storm.

Nirmala's eloquence in recounting her experiences is matched only by her humility and deep spiritual insight. She opens her heart to the reader, allowing us to witness the intimate ways in which God's providence shaped her path. Each chapter is a reflection of the divine tapestry woven through her life, demonstrating that even in our darkest hours, God's presence is ever near, His guidance ever sure.

This book is not merely a recounting of past events; it is a beacon of hope, a wellspring of encouragement for all who find themselves navigating the complexities of life. Nirmala's testimony serves as a powerful reminder that God's grace is sufficient, His strength made perfect in our weakness.

I believe that readers will find themselves not only uplifted but also deeply inspired to reflect on their own spiritual journeys. Nirmala's experiences challenge us to see beyond the immediate struggles and to recognize the hand of God at work, molding and shaping us for His purposes.

It is my prayer that this book will serve as a source of strength and encouragement to many, guiding them towards a deeper faith and a renewed trust in God's unchanging promises. May Nirmala's story remind us all that no matter the depth of our trials, we are never alone, for God is with us, leading us towards His divine plan.

In the spirit of faith and hope,

Rev. Dr. Sebestian Ravi Kumar

Senior Pastor, Richmond Town Methodist Church | District Superintendent, Bangalore District | Assistant Executive Secretary, Bangalore Regional Conference, The Methodist Church in India

Dedication

It gives me great pleasure to present my book, *My Little Basket of Gratitudes*. While I first shared these words in the presence of our dear pastors and congregation in the holy sanctuary, I now offer this book to you, the reader. Whether you are in your home, among friends, or seeking inspiration, I hope these pages bring you comfort and help you find your own little basket of gratitude.

I feel as though I am presenting my child to be baptized, standing before God with the assurance and promise that I will nurture the little one in His knowledge and wisdom. After many days of waiting, God has enabled me to bring this book to you, so that together we may glorify and praise His holy name.

This book is not meant to be stocked on a shelf, at least, not permanently. Of course, you may place it there for a time, but I hope you will give it a special place in the shelves of your heart. Turn to its pages daily, even if just for a moment, to recollect and give thanks for the immeasurable gifts God has showered upon us.

God's blessings and grace never come to an end; they are new every morning. *My Little Basket of Gratitudes* is nothing but a reflection of the many blessings poured upon us, whether we are aware of them or not. Sometimes, we are ignorant of the countless small blessings heaped upon us every moment, blessings without which we could not survive for even a single minute. The air we breathe, the act of walking, talking, moving our hands and legs freely, even the involuntary activities that happen within us, are all gifts we often take for granted.

We walk away from these blessings as if we are entitled to them, just as the nine lepers in the Bible, healed by Jesus, did not return to give thanks, thinking it was their right to be healed. But just hold your breath for a few seconds and feel the discomfort. Imagine if your hands or legs were fixed in one position forever, how would your life be? Would it still feel worth living?

God, in His wonderful knowledge, power, and wisdom, has equipped us with every comfort. As the Psalmist David said in Psalm 103, we must continually remind ourselves to bless the Lord with all that is within us and never forget all His benefits - not just the big and visible ones, but all benefits, big and small, visible and invisible. He forgives all our iniquities, heals all our diseases, lifts us from the pit, crowns us with loving kindness and mercy, and satisfies us with good things so that our youth is renewed like the eagle's.

This little book is a mirror, reflecting ourselves, our virtues and vices, gradually unfolding as we turn its pages. It is a school for correcting ourselves, for we have often compromised with the truth. I hope this little book will inspire and encourage you to recognize the intricacies of your own life.

I want to end with a heartfelt quote in Hindi:

जीवन और कुछ भी नहीं, तेरी मेरी कहानी है
जिसका हर पन्ना उसकी कृपा की निशानी है
प्यार का दर्पण है, जिसे हम सबको दिखाना है
हम उसके बगीचे के फूल हैं, जिसकी रूह हमें दुनिया में फैलानी है
जिसने अपना सब कुछ हमारे लिए न्योछावर कर दिया

All Glory be to God!

Nirmala Roop Singh

1

We are the Apple of His Eye

We live in an apartment complex with plenty of space to walk and move about. There are special areas for tiny tots, playful toddlers, and older children, as well as wide walking paths for people like me - the elderly who need a gentle stroll and a steady companion.

At seventy-five, with a collection of ailments earned over the years, I rely on my caretaker to accompany me on these daily walks. Sometimes, as I lace up my shoes and prepare to step outside, I remember the days when I could walk briskly on my own, without a second thought. Now, each outing is a small victory, a reminder of both my limitations and the grace that allows me to keep moving forward. I have learned to appreciate these moments, even when my body aches, because they connect me to the world beyond my four walls.

As we make our way around the grounds, I'm greeted by the joyful sounds of children at play. It is a delight to watch them - some are accompanied by their grandparents, others by attentive nannies. Their laughter fills the air, a reminder that life's simple pleasures are often the sweetest. Sometimes, I pause on a bench and simply watch, letting their happiness wash over me. It brings back memories of my own children, Roshan and Christabel, when they were little - how I'd watch over them with the same mix of love and worry, always alert for a scraped knee or a sudden tumble.

I am especially drawn to the way the caretakers and grandparents watch over the little ones. Their eyes rarely leave the children, always alert, always ready. When a toddler wriggles free from a guiding hand, the adult's posture changes instantly - more vigilant, sometimes breaking into a gentle run to catch up. There is a quiet determination in their movements, a silent promise to protect, to prevent a stumble or a fall. I see myself in those watchful elders, remembering how fiercely I wanted to shield my loved ones from every hurt, even when I knew I couldn't always be there.

I witness these small, everyday acts of care and my thoughts drift towards scripture. I remember the words from Deuteronomy 32:10, where it is written that God cared for Jacob as the "apple of His eye." How comforting it is to know that if we, with our human limitations, care so deeply for our children and grandchildren, how much more must our Heavenly Father care for us? The verse tells us that God found Jacob in a desert land, in a howling wilderness. He shielded him, cared for him, and guarded him as the apple of His eye.

This truth fills me with awe. God's care extends to every living creature—from the tiniest worm to the largest mammoth—and especially to us, made in His image. If we are so diligent in watching over our loved ones, how much more vigilant is God in watching over each of us? I think back to the many times in my own life when I felt lost or afraid—during illness, after loss, or simply in the quiet hours of the night—and I realize that I was never truly alone. Even when I could not see the path ahead, I was being watched over, guided, and protected by a love greater than my own.

As I finish my walk, I carry this reflection in my heart. Surrounded by laughter, love, and the watchful eyes of caretakers, I am reminded that we are all under the gaze of a loving God who shields, sustains, and cherishes us. Each day, as I step out into the world, I do so with gratitude, knowing that I am the apple of His eye.

All glory be to God!

2

Gratitude for the Everyday

Today, I want to present you with a beautiful flower from my basket of gratitude - for the benefit of all of us, and to the glory of God.

As I go about my daily life, I often find myself counting the small blessings that many people might overlook: the simple act of breathing, the refreshment of a glass of water, the ability to step outside and feel the sun on my face. Sometimes, I wonder if others might question what is so special about these things. After all, these are gifts that everyone receives, not just me. Why, then, should I give special thanks to God for what is shared by all?

I remember a time, not so long ago, when even these simple things were not guaranteed for me. During my treatment for breast cancer, there were days when every breath felt hard-won, and a sip of water was a small victory. In those moments, I realized how precious these "ordinary" blessings truly are. Now, every time I take a deep breath or enjoy a cup of tea, I am reminded of God's mercy and grace.

When such thoughts cross my mind, I am drawn to the story from Luke 17:11-19. In this passage, Jesus heals ten lepers after they cry out to Him for mercy. Yet, only one returns to thank Him. Jesus asks, "Were not all ten cleansed? Where are the other nine?"

The nine who did not return were Jews, and perhaps they felt entitled to their healing - that it was their right, and so there was no need to express gratitude. But the one who came back to thank Jesus was a Samaritan, someone considered an outsider. He recognized that he was unworthy, and so he returned, overflowing with gratitude.

This story resonates deeply with me. I have learned, especially in my later years, that gratitude is not just for the extraordinary moments, but for the everyday gifts that sustain us. None of us are truly worthy, yet God's bountiful gifts are poured out on us each day. I try to make it a habit to pause, reflect, and thank God for the small mercies as well as the great ones. Whether it's a kind word from a neighbor, a phone call from my children, or simply the strength to get out of bed, I see each as a flower in my basket of gratitude.

Let us always remember to return to Him with grateful hearts, acknowledging His grace in every moment. May we never take His blessings for granted, but instead, cherish them, big and small, with humility and thankfulness.

All glory be to God!

3

A Dark Valley Experience

My Testimony in Richmond Town Methodist Church, October 29, 2023

I stand before you and before the Almighty God a heart full of gratitude and humility, eager to praise His name and testify to His unfailing kindness.

I am Nirmala Roop Singh, wife of the late Mr. Vincent Roop Singh, whom many of you, especially fellow senior citizens and some younger friends, may remember. Losing Vincent to COVID-19 on December 11, 2021, was like having the ground swept out from beneath me. He was not just my husband, but my mentor - spiritually, mentally, and emotionally. His wisdom shaped my days, and his quiet strength was the anchor of our home. When he left, I felt as if the sun had set on my life. I remember waking up in the mornings, expecting to hear his voice or see his smile, only to be met by a silence that echoed through every room. The loneliness was overwhelming, and there were days when I wondered if I would ever feel whole again.

In those darkest days, when grief threatened to swallow me, I clung to the promises in scripture. A still, small voice from Psalm 27 whispered to my heart: "He will keep me safe in His dwelling in the day of trouble; He will hide me in the shelter of His tabernacle and set me high upon a rock." I would sit by the window, letting the sunlight warm my face, and repeat those words to myself, sometimes through tears. Slowly, I began to feel God's presence as a gentle comfort, reminding me that I was never truly alone.

Just as I was beginning to find my footing, another trial arrived. In August 2022, I was struck by severe leg pain. I could not take a single step without my son's support. I remember the frustration of losing my independence and the fear that my world was shrinking further. When the doctors diagnosed me with thrombectomy and found blockages in my arteries, I was terrified. Two surgeries within twenty days felt like more than I could bear. Yet, in the hospital, as I lay waiting, I found myself praying - not for miracles, but for the, but for the courage to face whatever came next. I pictured God holding my hand, steadying me when I was weak.

After the surgeries, I thought the worst was behind me. But in February 2023, I received the diagnosis of breast cancer. I was stunned. I remember sitting in the doctor's office, my mind racing, my heart pounding. "Why, Father? Why me, O Lord?" I cried out in prayer, feeling as if wave after wave was crashing over me. But then, once again, God's Word came to came to me, this time from Isaiah 41:10: "Fear not, I am with you; do not be dismayed, for I am your God. I will strengthen you and help you; I will uphold you with my righteous right hand." Those words became my lifeline.

Radiation treatments were gruelling. Each session felt like a walk through the valley of the shadow of death. The sterile smell of the hospital, the coldness of the machines, the uncertainty of each outcome - it was all so overwhelming. Yet, in those moments, I would close my eyes and imagine Jesus reaching out to rescue me, just as He would the lost sheep. The words of Psalm 23 comforted me: "I fear no evil, for Thou art with me; Thy rod and Thy staff, they comfort me."

The mastectomy in April 2023 was another mountain to climb. The physical pain was matched only by the emotional toll. Losing my hair and the physical changes to my body were difficult to accept. I grieved not just for my health, but for the woman I once saw in the mirror. During my hospital stay, I contracted a urinary tract infection that left me drained and unable to eat. The doctors urged me to eat, but even the smallest bite felt impossible.

I remembered the image of a golden retriever, obediently waiting for his master's command before eating. It struck me then how dependent we are on God for even the most basic things. Having food before me but being unable to eat was a humbling lesson. I realized anew that not even a blade of grass moves without God's will.

Shortly after my surgery, I suffered a bad fall in my room, requiring nine stitches and a month of recovery. There were moments when I wondered if my body would ever heal. Yet, through every setback, I sensed God's gentle encouragement, reminding me to be patient with myself.

Now, eighteen months after these trials began, I look back and see not only the pain and loss, but also the incredible ways God has sustained me. My children, Roshan and Christabel, have been my pillars - Roshan just a call away, Christabel always close by. Their love and presence have been a daily reminder of God's faithfulness. My extended family, friends, and pastors have prayed for me without ceasing. I am deeply grateful for their love and support, which have carried me through the darkest nights.

I have lost much—my hair, my beauty, my former energy—but I have never lost the love of God or His presence in my life. Through every circumstance, His promise has held me fast. I often reflect on Isaiah 40:29–31: "He gives power to the weak, and to those who have no might He increases strength… They shall mount up with wings like eagles; they shall run and not be weary, they shall walk and not faint." These words give me hope that, in time, I will be renewed in strength and courage, ready to serve God in whatever way He calls.

If there is one thing I've learned, it is this: even in the most barren deserts, God's presence is enough. His love is the shelter in my storm, and His promises are the light that guides me home.

All glory be to God!

4

Halloween, Little Hands and Full Bags

"Ask and it shall be given to you; seek and you shall find; knock and the door will be opened to you."

– Matthew 7:7-8

At my age, I've learned that an afternoon nap is one of life's greatest pleasures - right up there with a hot cup of tea and a good book. But as any grandparent knows, a suspicious silence in a house with grandchildren is rarely a sign of peace. Sure enough, I woke up to the sound of giggles and the unmistakable feeling that something was afoot.

In marched Jake and Gia, my two little whirlwinds, faces covered in a wild mess of squiggles, dots, and what looked suspiciously like my eyeliner. I had to stifle a laugh, though I'm sure my eyes were twinkling. "What on earth happened to your faces?" I asked, trying to sound stern but failing miserably.

"Nani! Today is Halloween!" they declared, their eyes shining brighter than the Diwali diyas. They excitedly explained their plan to join their friends and visit every flat in the building, collecting chocolates from all the neighbors. I could barely get a word in before they dashed off, leaving behind a trail of face paint and anticipation.

A couple of hours later, back they came, each clutching a little cloth bag - the kind we usually use for coconuts at weddings, mind you. But today, those bags were overflowing with chocolates, biscuits, cookies, and enough sugar to keep them bouncing off the walls for a week.

I looked at their loot, amazed. "Did you pay for all this?" I asked, raising an eyebrow.

They shook their heads, grinning from ear to ear. "No, Nani!"

Well, I saw my chance. "You know, this reminds me of something from the Bible," I said, settling into my storyteller's chair. "Matthew 7:7-8 says, 'Ask and it shall be given to you; seek and you shall find; knock and the door will be opened to you.' Just look at you two! You knocked on doors, you asked, and now your bags are full. Sometimes, all it takes is a little faith…and perhaps a clever costume."

I went on to explain that just as our neighbors filled their bags with goodies, God fills our lives with good things when we ask with trust and sincerity. "But remember," I added, eyeing their stash, "God also loves a cheerful giver. So, how about sharing a chocolate or two with your dear old Nani?"

They looked at each other, then at their bags, and after a long, dramatic pause, shook their heads in unison. "No, Nani! These are for us!"

Ah, children! Always quick to receive, but a little slower to give. I just chuckled and said, "Well, God gives us air, water, and even His only Son freely. Surely, we can share our blessings with others, too."

All glory be to God!

5

If God Be For Us

Testimony given on my 75th birthday to a small gathering of family and friends

Looking back over the years, I am often amazed at how God's hand has guided and protected our family through every trial. Ours was a family of seven - my parents, both teachers, and us five children. The eldest was my sister, just 13 at the time, followed by my brother at 11, then three younger girls: one aged five, another just a year and nine months, and the youngest, a tiny one-month-old infant.

Because my parents were teachers, we moved often, packing up our lives and settling wherever their next posting took us. One such transfer brought us to Tarikere, a town with a predominantly Hindu community. Finding a place to stay was not easy, but eventually, my parents managed to rent a large house. No sooner had we moved in than neighbors came by, their faces full of concern. They warned us that the house was haunted, that previous tenants had seen "ghosts" moving about. My parents were shocked, but they took courage from the scriptures - especially Romans 8:31-39:

"If God be for us, who can be against us? He who did not spare His own Son, but delivered Him up for us all, how shall He not with Him also freely give us all things?"

Days went by, but not a single ghost made its presence known. We were never bothered by anything supernatural. My parents clung to God's promises in Psalms 91:7-8:

"A thousand may fall at your side, ten thousand at your right hand, but it will not come near you. You will only look with your eyes and see the punishment of the wicked."

As my mother had to teach, she sometimes left the two youngest children in the care of my five-year-old sister. Imagine that - such a tiny girl, left responsible for her baby sisters! The school was kind enough to let my mother check on us often, but still, it was a lot to ask of a child. I'm told that whenever the babies cried, my brave five-year-old sister would tie a rope to the cradle and sit outside, rocking the baby from a distance. She was scared, but she did her best.

Looking back, I see God's protection in every detail. Despite the odds, our family was kept safe, provided for, and shielded from harm. And that little one-month-old infant? That was me - now 76 years old, Mrs. Nirmala Roop Singh. The courageous five-year-old caretaker was my sister, Mrs. Doruthy Sunanda Raj, now 80. Our eldest sister, Ms. Elizabeth, was the backbone of our family, carrying the burdens of our parents and even choosing to remain unmarried so she could support us all. She passed away at the age of 76 and a half, and it was my privilege to care for her in her later years.

Our journey took us to many places, including Sringeri, a renowned seat of Brahmin culture and the Goddess Sharadamba. As children, we joined our friends at the temple, played by the calm banks of the Tunga River, and fed puffed rice to the eager fish. We even participated in local festivals - bathing in the river, putting kumkum on our foreheads, and joining in the pradakshinas around the deity. During Ganesh festivals, we offered garike grass to the idols and sometimes decorated our own plates for the aarati procession.

Through all these experiences, God guided my parents to keep us faithful to Jesus Christ alone, despite the many influences around us. That is something I deeply admire about my parents, Mr. L.N. Paul Satyarthi and Mrs. Manoharamma, and for which I thank God for his mercy.

As we grew up witnessing the hardships our family faced, my immediate elder sister, Mrs. Shantha Kumari (now nearly 77 years), and I decided to shoulder the family's responsibilities as soon as we finished our college education. God, in His faithfulness, provided us with good jobs and a future.

Looking back, I see only God's grace and protection over our lives.

All glory be to God!

6

The Wise Builder's Secret

"The rains came down and the floods went up, and the wind blew and beat against the house, but it did not fall, because it had its foundation on the rock."

– Matthew 7:25

I still remember my very first visit to a beach, even though it happened many years ago. The excitement I felt was almost childlike as my husband and I made our way onto the soft, golden sand. The sea breeze was cool and refreshing, and the rhythmic sound of the waves was music to my ears. Hand in hand, we walked along the shoreline, our feet sinking gently into the wet sand. I was absolutely delighted when the gentle waves rolled over my feet, cool and invigorating, as if the ocean itself was welcoming us with a playful kiss.

But that pleasant moment didn't last long. Before we knew it, the waves grew larger and more forceful, lashing at our feet with renewed vigor. With each wave, we felt the sand beneath us begin to shift and give way. What had seemed so solid and stable just moments before was suddenly unreliable, and we found ourselves struggling to keep our balance. We gripped each other's hands more tightly, trying not to fall as the ground literally slipped away beneath us.

In that moment of instability, a verse from the Bible came to mind - Matthew 7:24-27. It tells the story of two builders: one wise, who built his house on the rock, and one foolish, who built his house on the sand. When the rains fell, the floods rose, and the winds blew, only the house built on the rock stood firm. The house built on sand, however, collapsed with a great crash.

That experience at the beach was a vivid reminder of a deeper spiritual truth. Life, much like the sea, is unpredictable. Sometimes we think we are standing on solid ground—our plans, our achievements, our relationships—only to find that when the storms of life come, these foundations can quickly wash away. Doubts, disappointments, losses, and frustrations can hit us like furious waves, threatening to sweep us off our feet.

But as I've learned over the years, we have a foundation that is truly unshakable. When we place our trust in God—our rock, our refuge, and our strength - we can withstand even the fiercest storms. His promises, provisions, and protection are the solid ground beneath our feet. When society's pressures, criticisms, or temptations threaten to pull us down, God upholds us with His righteous right hand and helps us stand firm.

Standing on that shifting sand, I realized how easy it is to rely on things that do not last. But when we build our lives on God's

Word and His faithfulness, we are like the wise builder whose house remains standing, no matter how hard the storms rage. So, whenever doubts assail or troubles come crashing in, remember: stand firm on the rock of God's love, mercy, and promises. He will never let you fall.

All glory be to God!

7

A Mother's Love In the Face of Darkness

A most heinous crime of a woman CEO murdering her own son, an innocent four-year-old child on the 7th of January 2024, has been making the rounds in the newspapers every day. The nation is shocked, people are horrified, children are terrified, and humanity is sinking under the debris of cruelty. This atrocious act was committed by a woman who was also a so called "mother", whose love and kindness have been praised since time immemorial.

However, she is not the first to exhibit such a mental disorder, nor will she be the last. Here is another story, mentioned in the Bible, that highlights the kind heart of a mother who was willing to give up her motherhood for the sake of her child's life. The story is narrated in 1 Kings 3:16–28.

The story goes like this: Once, two prostitutes came to King Solomon to seek justice. One woman said that they both lived in the same house, and she gave birth to a son while she was there. On the third day, the other woman also gave birth to a son. One night, the second woman's son died because she accidentally lay on him. She claimed that the other woman got up in the middle of the night, took her living son from beside her while she was sleeping, and placed the dead child at her breast. When she awoke in the morning, she realized that the child beside her was not the one she had borne. But the other woman insisted, saying, *"No, the living child is mine, and the dead one is yours."*

King Solomon then ordered a sword to be brought and commanded that the living boy be divided in two and given to both women. The second woman agreed, saying the boy would belong to neither of them. But the woman whose son was alive pleaded with the king, filled with compassion, and begged him to give the living boy to the other woman and not to kill him. Recognizing her genuine motherly love, Solomon ordered that the living boy be given to the first woman, declaring that she was his true mother.

Reflecting on these two episodes, my mind swiftly turned to a passage in the Old Testament - Isaiah 49:15–17 - which says, *"Can a woman forget her nursing child, or have no compassion for the child of her womb? But I will not forget you. See, I have inscribed you on the palms of my hands."*

What a powerful, great, and consoling assurance from our God - that He has carved our names on the palms of His hands, and He will never forget us. It is a spring of joy in this parched world.

8

Losing Our Daughter and Finding God's Mercy

"For the Son of Man came to seek and to save the lost."
– Luke 19:10

Some memories, no matter how many years pass, remain vivid in the heart. One such memory for me is from 1987, when our family set off on a South Indian tour with Asian Travels. It was an organized tour, and most of our stops were temple towns, each with its own history and grandeur. We didn't mind visiting these temples, especially since their architecture was so magnificent. One of the highlights was the famous Meenakshi Temple in Madurai.

The temple is enormous, with several entrances and a maze of corridors. Our daughter was just six years old at the time, and our son was nine and a half. We made sure to keep them close, holding their little hands as we wandered through the temple, taking in the sights. Inside, the temple was bustling with activity. Devotees moved about, some making offerings to the deity, others participating in what looked like auctions of jewelry and other valuables. The whole place felt more like a lively marketplace than a house of worship. It reminded me of the scene from the Bible when Jesus rebuked the money changers, saying, "You have made my Father's house a den of robbers."

As we wandered, marveling at the grandeur and commotion, we must have become too absorbed in our surroundings. At some point, without realizing it, we let go of the children's hands. Each of us was walking independently, lost in our own observations. Suddenly, a wave of panic washed over me as I realized the children were no longer by our side. My heart raced as we looked around, but all we could see were crowds of people, each preoccupied, moving briskly from one corner to another.

We dashed through the throngs, calling out for our children. By God's grace, we soon spotted our son. Relief flooded through me as we caught hold of him. We quickly instructed him to look for his sister in a particular direction, while my husband and I split up, searching frantically. Thankfully, my husband found our daughter standing alone in one of the temple's endless corridors. The poor child looked utterly bewildered, her small face streaked with confusion and fear. Surrounded by towering pillars and passageways that all seemed to look alike, she must have felt completely lost, every corner a mirror image of the last. The noise and bustle of the crowd only added to her distress.

The relief and gratitude we felt in that moment are impossible to describe. We knew, deep in our hearts, that God had watched over our precious child and, in His mercy, brought our family safely back together.

Even now, I shudder to think what could have happened if we hadn't found them in that vast, unfamiliar place. Truly, God was gracious, holding our children in the hollow of His hand and restoring our most precious gifts to us.

This whole episode reminded me of the parables in Luke 15 - the lost coin, the lost sheep, and the prodigal son. In each story, there is great rejoicing when what was lost is found. As it says in Luke 15:10, *"There is joy in the presence of God over one sinner who repents."* We too rejoiced, grateful for God's protection and mercy.

All glory be to God!

9

A Stranger's Kindness, A Mother's Relief

It's hard to believe, but our daughter managed to get lost a second time that very same year. I suppose some children are magnets for adventure - or perhaps for angels. This time, it happened after a prayer meeting I attended with both children. The plan was simple enough: we would all attend the meeting, have lunch together, and then my son would drop his little sister at my friend's house nearby before heading home himself. Our home, my friend's house, and the prayer meeting venue were all within walking distance, so I didn't think twice.

After lunch, I said my goodbyes and reminded my son to make sure his sister got safely to my friend's place. He did just as he was told, escorting her right up to the door. But when they knocked, no one answered. The house was locked, and my friend was nowhere to be found. My son, thinking he had done his duty, left her there and headed home.

Left alone, my daughter knocked and knocked, but still, no one came. Unsure what to do, she retraced her steps until she reached the main road. There, at a roundabout where several roads converged, she stood and stood, tears welling up in her eyes, completely lost and not knowing which way to turn. She didn't know the exact address, only the locality, and the streets all looked the same to her.

As she stood there, frightened and confused, a stranger noticed her distress. He approached gently and asked where she wanted to go. All she could muster was the name of our area, not the road. Taking pity on her, this kind man led her in the right direction. She later told us she couldn't remember exactly how they found our house—she probably recognized the roads as they got closer, and eventually, with the stranger escorting her, she arrived home safely.

By the time I returned home that evening, my mother-in-law was waiting for me, surrounded by other family members. She asked, "Where is Neetu?" I replied confidently that she was at my friend's house and would be home soon. But then my mother-in-law called Neetu from the other room, and there she was, safe and sound. We asked her what happened, and she told us about the locked door, her tears at the crossroads, and the kind stranger who helped her find her way.

I immediately asked if anyone had taken the man's name or phone number so I could thank him, but no one had. In those days, we didn't have mobile phones, and the man never appeared again. To this day, I firmly believe he was an angel sent by God to protect our daughter - a shelter from the storm and a shade from the heat, as it says in Isaiah 25:4.

We are forever grateful to God and to that mysterious stranger, though I regret never being able to thank him in person.

All glory be to God!

10

God's Hand in the Little Things

It was on October 4, 2023, when we made our way to Apollo Hospital for what was supposed to be a routine check - up. My son and my caretaker accompanied me, as they always do for such visits. These hospital trips have become a part of life in my later years, and I am grateful for the support and care my family gives me. We were first guided to the area where they took my vital readings - blood pressure, sugar, and all the usual parameters. After that, we were asked to wait for the doctor. Waiting rooms always seem to stretch time, and that day was no different. We waited for about an hour before our turn finally came.

Once inside, the doctor examined me thoroughly. He smiled and said everything looked perfect, though he did remind me, as always, to eat properly and take care of my diet. Then, almost as an afterthought, he suggested we consult a nephrologist. That suggestion made me a little anxious. At my age, any mention of kidneys or specialists is enough to set the mind racing. I remember silently praying, asking God to protect me from any hidden troubles. By God's grace, the nephrologist checked me and found nothing amiss. My heart was light with relief, and I silently offered a prayer of thanks.

After the consultations, we were told to wait again for the reports. It was then that my caretaker suddenly realized my mobile phone was missing. She checked her bag, I checked mine, and my son searched his backpack, but it was nowhere to be found. For a moment, a wave of worry swept over us. In today's world, a mobile phone holds so much: contacts, messages, precious photos, and a sense of connection to loved ones.

Without hesitation, my caretaker hurried back to the area where we had been earlier. Those five minutes felt like an eternity to me. I sat there, praying silently, hoping for good news. Then, to my immense relief, she returned, beaming, with my mobile phone in her hand. She had found it sitting right on the table where the nurse had taken my readings, untouched.

We all rejoiced at getting my mobile back and thanked God profusely for restoring it to us. It wasn't just about the phone itself, but the trouble and distress we would have faced if it had truly been lost - especially for my son, who always worries about me. What felt truly miraculous was that the phone was found in a place where hundreds of people pass by every hour. It could so easily have fallen into the wrong hands, but I believe God's angels were watching over it. I rejoiced, just as the owner of the lost sheep, the lost coin, and the lost son rejoiced in Luke 15:3-32. God is gracious, even in the smallest of matters.

All glory be to God!

11

Losing Our Son and Finding God's Unfailing Grace

Perhaps it is true that those who are deeply rooted in faith and the Word of God are tested the most—just as Job and Paul were, time and again. Ordinary people like us also face many trials on our journey of faith, and sometimes those tests shake us to our very core.

It was in the year 2000 that we faced the greatest trial of our lives. Our son failed his P.U.C. exams and was utterly devastated. We tried to reassure him, telling him not to worry and to try again the following year. We enrolled him in coaching classes, and soon enough, the day of the next examination arrived.

That morning, I encouraged my son to be bold and do his best. I told him to wait for me at the exam venue after he finished, and I would come pick him up. After a short prayer together, he left for the exam. The test was scheduled from 9AM to 12 noon. I reached the college promptly at noon and waited for him to come out. One by one, all the boys exited the hall, but my son was nowhere to be seen.

Panic began to set in. I went inside and found the invigilator, who was collecting the answer sheets. I showed him my son's hall ticket and asked if he had already left. The invigilator checked and told me that my son was marked absent. Shocked and anxious, I rushed home, hoping he had returned there. But he was not at home either. My heart felt heavy with fear.

I tried to calm myself and waited for my husband to return. When he came home, he too was shocked. We waited anxiously until late at night, then informed our siblings. They advised us to lodge a police complaint, as did our pastor. We went to the Ulsoor Gate police station and filed a report, then returned home and prayed together. This was on the 3rd of April. There was no news of our son until the 6th of April. Those days were filled with worry and helplessness, but we tried to strengthen one another through prayer.

Then, at around 2 AM, we received a phone call from our pastor, Rev. Arun Andrews. He told us that our son was at the gate of Philomena Hospital and that we should come and take him home. Our hearts leapt with relief and gratitude. My husband's brother—a huge strength for us—came with us, and when we saw our son, we rejoiced and took him straight to Martha's Hospital for a check - up and some much - needed care.

Later, our son told us that he had attempted to end his life three times in those three days, but by God's grace, he had not succeeded. We firmly believe that God protected him in His tabernacle during those days of trouble. This experience reminds me of the promise in Jeremiah 29:11-12: *"For surely I know the plans I have for you, says the Lord, plans for your welfare and not for harm, to give you a future with hope…"* God truly restored our precious son to us amidst chaos and hardship. We rejoiced as the owners of the lost coin, the lost sheep, and the prodigal son rejoiced, and I am sure there was rejoicing in heaven as well.

All glory be to God!

12

Reunited in the City of Lights

It was in 2003 that I won what I can only call the lottery of my life—a week - long trip to Europe for two, courtesy of Costa Cruise. The story began quite simply. In December 2002, my son and I were shopping at Shoppers Stop near Garuda Mall. I bought him a pair of shoes and jeans, and the salesman handed me a slip to fill out with my address and phone number. I filled it in and promptly forgot all about it.

A month later, I received a call from Shoppers Stop, informing me that I was one of three lucky winners of a ticket for two to coastal Europe, with free travel and stay on the Costa Cruise for a week. What a blessing! My husband was just as thrilled, and we both thanked God for such a bountiful gift.

The cruise itself was an unforgettable experience. We were allotted a cabin on the third floor of the ship, with a wonderful view of the serene, blue sea. The Costa ship was a world in itself—we could walk, play, watch movies, dine, and even dance as we sailed. The ship had multiple floors, all open for us to explore. Whenever the ship docked, we had the chance to visit cities like Milan, Geneva, parts of Belgium, and even a bit of Germany. After the cruise, we spent another week at our own expense, enjoying even more sights.

Paris, with its famous Eiffel Tower on the banks of the Seine, was a highlight of our journey. We made friends with people from all over the world and enjoyed every stop along the way. When we reached Paris, we were awestruck by the magnificent structure of the Eiffel Tower. We even took a boat ride on the river, soaking in the beauty of the city and its surroundings.

But then came a moment of anxiety. Around 7 PM in the evening, it was time to return to our bus. My husband and I decided to quickly visit the restroom, but there was a queue, and by the time we returned, our bus and fellow travelers were nowhere to be seen. For a moment, we wondered what to do. My husband suggested we hire a taxi back to the hotel, but I felt certain that our guide or someone from our group would come looking for us. After all, the group leader was responsible for everyone's safety.

We decided to wait near a police post so we could be easily found. The policeman was kind and helpful, and after a little while, we saw our guide and some group members approaching us. What a relief it was to be reunited! No one scolded us; perhaps they could see the worry on our faces. They simply held our hands and led us back to the bus.

Reflecting on that day, I am filled with gratitude for the way God led us safely through unfamiliar places and brought us back to our group. I am reminded of Psalm 32:6-8: "You are a hiding place for me; you preserve me from trouble; you surround me with glad cries of deliverance."

Truly, thanks and glory be to God!

13

Angels Always on Duty

It was in October, 2023, that I once again truly witnessed the hand of God protecting my loved ones. That afternoon, our housemaid, Deepa, was taking my two grandchildren to the football ground in J.P. Nagar. They set off in an auto rickshaw, excited for an afternoon of play, never imagining how close they would come to disaster.

As they were making their way through the busy streets, a tempo suddenly came speeding out from an adjacent road and crashed into the auto. The impact was so severe that the entire right side of the auto was badly bruised, and the front glass shattered into countless pieces. I can only imagine the shock and terror that must have swept over Deepa and the children in that moment. When I later saw their faces, they were still numb, speechless, and utterly bewildered by what had happened.

But here is the miracle: not a single scratch was found on any of them. Despite the damage to the vehicle, my grandchildren and

Deepa walked away completely unharmed. It was as if invisible hands had shielded them from all harm.

In that moment, the words of Psalm 91 came rushing to my mind: *"You will not fear the terror of the night, or the arrow that flies by day… On their hands they (the angels) will bear you up, so that you will not dash your foot against a stone."* How true these words proved to be for our family that day. Though danger was lurking so close, it could do nothing because of God's grace and protection.

I am reminded especially of Psalm 91:12: *"On their hands they (the angels) will bear you up, so that you will not dash your foot against a stone."* I am convinced that God's angels were present, bearing up my grandchildren and Deepa, just as the Psalm promises.

I am filled with gratitude, knowing how different things could have been.

Glory be to God for His constant watchfulness and loving care!

14

The Miracle of the Family Tree

After my husband passed on to glory on December 11, 2021, we needed to obtain a family tree certificate to complete some transactions regarding the sale of our apartment in Rajarajeshwari Nagar. On 10th May, Roshan and I went about this activity and approached the Nadakacheri office in Kengeri, near the bus stand, to apply for the Family Tree.

We submitted all the required documents and paid the official fee of Rs. 500. Just then, an agent approached us and, in what was clearly an attempt at bribery, suggested that for Rs. 7,000, the certificate could be ready in just four days. I must admit, I was tempted for a moment, thinking of all the time and hassle it might save us. I even tried to bargain with him for Rs. 3,000, but he wouldn't budge. In the end, conscience prevailed, and we decided to proceed through the official channel, trusting the process. The clerk assured us the certificate would be ready in 14 days.

We waited patiently for almost a month, but nothing happened. On June 7th, Roshan and I went back to Nadakacheri to check on the status of our application. They told us the application had been rejected due to missing details of family members. I was certain we had submitted everything they had asked for, but the clerk asked us to come back after two days so he could retrieve the file. He promised to call once he found it.

Two days passed, but there was no call. Roshan was busy, so I decided to go alone. I prayed that the Tahasildar would have a patient heart and listen to my plea. When I arrived, I saw the Tahasildar in his chamber and explained my situation. He called the clerk and asked him to bring my file. The officer told me not to worry and assured me he would take care of it. I thanked him and waited outside.

After about an hour and a half, I thought the work might not get done that day. Before leaving, I decided to check with the interior section of the office where the officials were working on their computers. The young man there told me he was working on my file and asked me to wait a few more minutes. At 1:30 PM, he came out and said he would show the papers to the Tahasildar. Within minutes, he returned and handed me the endorsed family tree certificate.

I could hardly believe the work was done so quickly and smoothly, and without any extra payment. I thanked God profusely and expressed my gratitude to the officer. I even wanted to give a small token of thanks to the office boy, but he refused, saying, "Madam, this was the boss's order, and I will not take anything."

Yes, on his boss's order, the work was done swiftly and without delay.

This experience reminded me that when God gives, He gives freely and abundantly. As it says in Luke 6:38: *"Give, and it will be given to you. A good measure, pressed down, shaken together, and running over, will be poured into your lap. For with the measure you use, it will be measured to you."*

All glory be to God!

15

Staying Connected and Abiding in Christ

At 76, I've learned that having a direct connection with God is essential if you want to achieve anything meaningful in life. The words of Jesus in John 15:4-6 have become especially precious to me:

"Abide in me, and I in you. As the branch cannot bear fruit by itself, unless it abides in the vine, neither can you, unless you abide in me. I am the vine, you are the branches. Whoever abides in me and I in him, he it is that bears much fruit, for apart from me you can do nothing."

I must admit, even at my age, I still make the simplest mistakes in my daily routine - mistakes that remind me just how important it is to stay connected to the source. Let me share a few:

- I'll carefully measure out the rice, put it in the cooker, and then promptly forget to switch the cooker on before walking away to do something else.

- I load up the washing machine with clothes, add the detergent, close the lid, and then forget to press the 'start' button.
- I plug my mobile phone in for charging but forget to turn on the switch at the wall.
- I put my food in the microwave to heat but somehow forget to press the button to actually start it.

It's funny how often these little things happen, but they carry a deeper lesson. In every case, I've done all the right steps, but without connecting to the source of power - electricity - nothing happens. The rice stays raw, the clothes stay dirty, the phone stays dead, and the food stays cold.

It's the same with our spiritual lives. We can do everything else right, but if we're not connected to God - our true source of energy and power - nothing truly fruitful will come of it.

Just as a plant withers without soil, a fish dies without water, a student fails without studying, a laborer earns nothing without working, and a lion does not eat without hunting, so too do we wither spiritually if we do not abide in Jesus. As the scripture says, "Whoever does not abide in me is thrown away like a branch and withers; such branches are gathered, thrown into the fire, and burned."

So, my prayer is simple: Lord, give us the grace and mercy to abide in you, to draw our strength and energy from you by keeping your commandments. Jesus also said, *"If you abide in me, and my words abide in you, ask whatever you wish, and it will be done for you." (John 15:7)*

Let us stay connected to the Source, for without Him, we can do nothing.

All glory be to God!

16

Jesus is Our Only Mediator

"For there is only one God, and only one mediator between God and mankind."

– 1 Timothy 2:5-6

These past months have tested my patience and faith in ways I never imagined. Our family has been caught in a legal tangle with our tenant, who refuses to vacate our flat even though her 11 - month agreement ended long ago. She continues to occupy our home unlawfully, and every polite request or reminder has fallen on deaf ears. The entire ordeal has been exhausting, emotionally and mentally. I often found myself wondering, "Where is justice in all this?"

When the court suggested mediation, I clung to a sliver of hope. Maybe, I thought, reason would prevail and the matter would be resolved fairly. But what happened next left me stunned and deeply frustrated. The tenant demanded six lakhs from us, claiming she had paid this amount to someone else just to enter our home. Not a single rupee of that money ever came to us, yet now she expects us to pay her to get our own property back! It was so unfair, so unreasonable, that I felt completely helpless.

What made it worse was the mediation court's attitude. Instead of taking action against her baseless demands, they simply asked us to reconsider our stance, as if we were the ones in the wrong. The very place where I expected justice seemed indifferent, and for a moment, I felt abandoned by the very system meant to protect us. The frustration and sense of injustice weighed heavily on my heart.

In my distress, I turned to God in prayer. I remembered that while earthly courts may fail, God never does. He alone is the true provider of justice. I found comfort in Psalm 128:1-2: *"You shall eat the fruit of the labor of your hands; you shall be happy, and it shall go well with you."* These words reminded me that God sees our struggles and will not let us be defeated by injustice.

As I prayed, a sense of relief and conviction washed over me. I realized that Jesus is our only true mediator, standing before God on our behalf. Earthly mediators may disappoint, but He never will. My heart is at peace, trusting that God's justice will prevail in His perfect time.

17

The Divine Invitation: "Come, Let Us Reason"

At 76, I've had plenty of time to think about life's big questions, and one thing that never ceases to amaze me is how God reaches out to us, even when we've gone astray. The words in Isaiah 1:18-20 have always touched me deeply:

"Come now, let us reason together, says the Lord: though your sins are like scarlet, they shall be as white as snow; though they are red like crimson, they shall become like wool. If you are willing and obedient, you shall eat the good of the land; But if you refuse and rebel, you shall be devoured by the sword; for the mouth of the Lord has spoken."

To me, these verses sound like a compromise call - a mediation offer from the Creator Himself. Imagine that: the great God of the universe, looking at us in our weakness and sin, and instead of turning away, He extends His powerful, loving hand and says, *"Come, let's talk this out."*

We humans have all fallen short of His glory. We stumble, struggle, and often find ourselves stuck in dark places, unable to climb out on our own. Yet, our merciful God doesn't leave us there. He calls us to Himself, not with condemnation, but with an invitation to reason together, to find a way forward.

What a wonderful God we have! Even while we were still sinners, He offered His only Son, Jesus, to die on the cross for our sake. Whoever believes in Him will not perish but have everlasting life. Can there be any greater love, kindness, or mercy than this? All He asks is that we accept His Son as our personal Saviour and King, and believe that He was raised from the dead. What a privilege!

But the offer doesn't stop there. God promises that whoever believes in Him will have the right to become His child and gain eligibility to enter His kingdom. What a sacrificial offer - what a divine compromise - extended by our all - powerful God to rescue us from the pit of sin.

So, as I reflect on these words, I am filled with gratitude. No matter how far we may wander, God's invitation remains: *"Come, let us reason together."*

All glory be to God!

18

It is God Who Provides the Growth

The flowers are in full bloom, swaying gently in the breeze, their colours bright and cheerful. It is such a delight to watch them. Only yesterday, I noticed some of these same flowers were just tiny buds, tightly closed and full of promise. Today, they have opened up, revealing all their beauty. It amazes me how quickly things can change and how life unfolds in its own time.

This simple act of tending to my garden often brings to mind a deeper truth. I am reminded of the words from 1 Corinthians 3:6-9: "*I planted the seed, Apollos watered it, but God gave the growth.*" In the early church, there were divisions among believers, some saying they followed Paul, others saying they followed Apollos. But Paul, in his wisdom, reminded them that neither the one who plants nor the one who waters is anything; it is God who makes things grow.

As I reflect on this, I realize that my role in the garden is much like my role in life and in faith. I can plant seeds, water them, and give them the best care I can, but I cannot force them to grow or blossom. That miracle belongs to God alone. In the same way, when we share kindness, encouragement, or the good news of Christ with others, we are simply planting and watering seeds in their hearts. The true growth, the transformation, comes from God.

Paul and Apollos were just helpers in God's great garden, co - workers in His field. We, too, are called to be faithful in our small tasks, trusting that God will bring about the increase. Someone once said, Rev. David Kim rightly put it along the lines of, *"Every human heart is a mission field, and every believer is a missionary."* How true that is! Our job is to sow seeds of love, water them with patience and prayer, and leave the rest to God.

As I look at my blooming garden, I am reminded that in every area of life, God is the real gardener. We are His co - workers, and the miracle of growth is always in His hands.

All glory be to God!

19

Just as I Have Loved You

Recently, I watched a video that touched me deeply and left me reflecting on my own life. In the video, a father was sitting in his living room, completely absorbed in a video game, his headphones shutting out the world. In the same room were his two young children and their mother, who was clearly in distress, clutching her chest and suffering silently. The youngest child, still in her pram, noticed her mother's pain but was too little to help. She tried everything she could to get attention - throwing her water bottle, tossing a small plant - but no one noticed.

Eventually, the older child saw her baby sister's distress and followed her gaze to their mother. Realizing something was wrong, she tried to get her father's attention, but he was so engrossed in his game that he didn't notice. Finally, the little girl went up to her father and pulled off his headphones. Startled and a bit annoyed, he finally looked up, saw the direction his daughter was pointing, and understood the seriousness of the situation.

In an instant, he rushed to his wife's side, giving her water and medicine, and helped her through her predicament. Afterwards, he threw aside his headphones and embraced his wife and children, overwhelmed with relief and love. Watching this scene, my heart melted. It was so moving to see family members come together, comforting and caring for one another in a moment of need.

But what struck me most was how much we are like that father at times. How often do we get so caught up in our own worlds—our routines, our hobbies, our worries—that we fail to notice the needs of those around us? Sometimes, it takes a jolt, a gentle tug from someone else, to remind us to look up and truly see.

Jesus commands us in John 13:34, *"Just as I have loved you, you must also love one another."* Love isn't just a feeling; it's an action, a choice to notice, to care, and to respond. Let us not be so distracted that we miss the opportunities to love—within our families and beyond. May we be quick to set aside our distractions and reach out with compassion, just as He has loved us.

20

The Tripod of Marriage: Love, Caring and Sharing

"Submit to one another out of reverence for Christ."

– Ephesians 5:21

The older I get, the more I realize how important relationships are in sustaining us through life's journey. Ephesians 5:21 calls husbands and wives to be subject to one another, a concept often misunderstood even among Christians. Many think submission means one person is less important than the other, but true submission is a mutual act of love and respect. In marriage, both husband and wife are called to submit to each other. For the wife, this means willingly following her husband's leadership in Christ, loving him, caring for him, and sharing life's joys and burdens. For the husband, it means putting aside his own interests to love, care for, and share with his wife.

I have learned that submission to one another is rarely a problem in Christian homes where both spouses have a strong relationship with Christ and where each is genuinely concerned for the other's happiness and well - being. Our Lord and Saviour Jesus Christ is the most beautiful and powerful model of this. Though He was God, He submitted His will to the Father, even to the point of death on the cross. What a picture of sacrificial obedience and love!

When I think of marriage, I often picture life as a tripod. The three legs are love, care, and sharing. On top sits the pot of sacrifice and kindness, and inside that pot is the gruel of goodness, faithfulness, and gentleness, cooked and served to all members of the family. If even one leg is missing, the tripod wobbles and the pot may fall. But when all three are strong, the family is nourished and sustained through every season.

In my own marriage, we have faced many challenges, but it was love, care, and a willingness to share that saw us through. We supported each other's dreams, comforted each other in sorrow, and celebrated together in joy. There were times of misunderstanding and hurt, but we always returned to the foundation of our faith and the call to submit to one another out of reverence for Christ.

As I reflect on these years, I am grateful for the gift of companionship and the lessons learned through both the easy and difficult times. My prayer is that every marriage would be built on these principles, so that each family may experience the sustaining power of relationships rooted in Christ.

All glory be to God!

21

A Time for Everything

> *"To everything there is a season, and a time to every purpose under the heaven."*
>
> *– Ecclesiastes 3:1*

Some years ago, I remember altering the side stitches of my blouses because they had become too tight for me. Now, those very same blouses hang loose on my shoulders. Time, as always, has taken its toll. This small change led my thoughts to the timeless words of Ecclesiastes: *"A time to plant and a time to pluck up what is planted, a time to kill and a time to heal..."* How true these words are! Life is a series of seasons, each with its own purpose and lesson.

God, in His wisdom, has set the rhythm of the world. As Daniel 2:21 says, *"He changes times and seasons; He removes kings and sets up kings; He gives wisdom to the wise and knowledge to those who have understanding."* Genesis 8:22 assures us that as long as the earth remains, *"seedtime and harvest, cold and heat, summer and winter, day and night, shall not cease."* Just as nature moves through its cycles, so do our lives.

I have come to see my own journey in terms of seasons. There have been winters - sadness, heartbreak, loneliness, and sickness. These were times when life felt cold and barren, yet even then, God's presence was a quiet comfort. Then came springs - full of hope, new beginnings, and fresh opportunities. Summers brought signs of growth, but also the need for protection and discernment amid life's distractions. Autumns were seasons of both achievement and failure, a time to gather the harvest and reflect on what had been sown.

Through all these seasons, I have learned to trust God's timing. Sometimes, I wished for spring when I was still in winter, or tried to hold onto summer when autumn was calling. But God, in His kindness, knows exactly what we need and when we need it. His support, faithfulness, goodness, mercy, and grace have carried me through every change.

As I altered my blouses, preparing them for whatever might come, another thought struck me: Am I exercising the same diligence in preparing my children for the seasons of their lives? The Bible speaks clearly about this responsibility.

In Deuteronomy 6:7, Moses instructs parents, *"You shall teach [God's laws] diligently to your children, and shall talk of them when you sit in your house, and when you walk by the way, and when you lie down, and when you rise."* Proverbs 19:18 reminds us, *"Discipline your children, for in that there is hope; do not be a willing party to their destruction."* And Proverbs 23:13-14 urges,

"Do not withhold discipline from a child… punish them with the rod and save them from death."

Just as we prepare for changing seasons in our own lives, we must lovingly guide our children, teaching them God's ways and preparing them for whatever lies ahead. May we embrace each season with gratitude, trusting that God's timing is perfect, and may we pass on this wisdom to the next generation.

All glory be to God!

22

The Wicked Will Not Prevail

"Do not fret because of evildoers or be envious of those who do wrong; for like the grass they will soon wither, like green plants they will soon die away."

– Psalm 37:1-2

One summer morning, I wandered through the yard of our garden, savoring the cool breeze that brushed across my face. It was one of those simple, perfect moments when nature itself seems to offer a blessing. As I walked, I watched the wind pick up dry leaves that had fallen on my path, spinning them in little circles before sweeping them away. The sight made me pause, and immediately my mind turned to the timeless words of Psalm 1.

"Blessed are those who do not follow the counsel of the wicked, or take the path that sinners tread, or sit in the seat of scoffers, but their delight is in the law of the Lord, and on His law they meditate day and night. They are like trees planted by streams of water, which yield their fruit in its season, and their leaves do not wither. In all

that they do, they prosper. The wicked are not so, but are like chaff that the wind drives away. Therefore, the wicked will not stand in the judgment, nor sinners in the congregation of the righteous. For the Lord watches over the way of the righteous, but the way of the wicked will perish."

How soothing these words are to my soul! The image of the wind driving away the chaff - the dry, useless husks - reminds me that the wicked, no matter how strong they may seem for a season, will ultimately be swept away. But those who root themselves in God's Word, who meditate on His law, are like sturdy trees by a riverbank, always nourished, always fruitful, and never withering, no matter the season.

In this world, we often see the wicked prosper, and it can be discouraging. But God's Word assures us that He sees everything, and He will act justly. The righteous need not fear, for the Lord Himself is their protector.

Psalm 91 echoes this promise of divine protection: *"He will deliver you from the snare of the fowler and from the deadly pestilence. He will cover you with His pinions, and under His wings you will find refuge… A thousand may fall at your side, ten thousand at your right hand, but it will not come near you… Because you have made the Lord your refuge, no evil shall befall you… For He will command His angels concerning you to guard you in all your ways."*

Psalm 37 also encourages us: *"Do not fret because of evildoers… Trust in the Lord and do good; so you will live in the land, and enjoy security."*

As I continued my walk, I felt a deep sense of peace. No matter what storms may come, or how the winds of trouble may blow, I know that God watches over the righteous. He is my refuge, my shield, and my strength. Like a tree by the water, I will stand firm, trusting in His promises.

All glory be to God!

23

Wide is the Gate and Broad is the Way

> *"Enter through the narrow gate. For wide is the gate and broad is the road that leads to destruction, and many enter through it. But small is the gate and narrow the road that leads to life, and only a few find it."*
>
> *– Matthew 7:13-14*

In the olden days, as I remember, door posts used to be short, and the lintel was set so low that I often wondered why it was made that way - forcing a person to bend in order to pass through. Later, I came to know that it was done purposefully. People were expected to show humility while entering the house and to demonstrate respect to the elders of the family.

As I pondered this, my mind wandered to the scripture in John 10:9-10, where Jesus says, "I am the door; if anyone enters by me, he will be saved and will go in and out and find pasture." My thoughts also went to Matthew 7:13-14, which says, "Enter by the narrow gate. For wide is the gate and broad is the road that leads to destruction, and many enter through it. But small is the gate and narrow the road that leads to life, and only a few find it."

How true this is! The world and its glamour are always calling out to us. We are constantly tempted to go along with the crowd, neglecting the narrow way that very few choose - a way that leads to true tranquillity and peace of mind. Instead, many prefer to follow the chaos and distractions of the world, lured by its temporary offers of happiness and fleeting peace.

That is why Jesus advises us to enter the Kingdom of Heaven by the narrow gate. It may not be the most popular or the easiest path, but it is the one that leads to real life, lasting peace, and eternal joy.

All glory be to God!

24

Rejoicing in Heaven

Luke 15:10 tells us, "I tell you, there is joy in the presence of the angels of God over one sinner who repents." This verse has always brought me great comfort and hope, especially as I reflect on the many "lost and found" stories that have touched my life and faith journey.

Recently, I had a remarkable experience that reminded me of this heavenly truth. After many years, I reconnected with a long - lost friend who had moved to another city. She was an avowed atheist, and though I had tried in the past to share with her about Jesus - His love, mercy, and the great sacrifice He made for us - she remained unconvinced. She was, as people say, a hard nut to crack. I would often pray for her, knowing that it is not in my hands to bring anyone to faith. I could only sow the seeds, speak of His goodness, and trust God to do the rest.

I remembered Paul's words about himself and Apollos: "We only sowed the seeds and watered them, but it is God who gives the growth." That truth comforted me, especially when my efforts seemed fruitless. I continued to pray, "Lord, only You can open her heart and help her understand the truth. Draw her to Yourself, in Your time and in Your way."

To my utter surprise and delight, when we met again after so many years, I found her much more open and responsive to the Word of God. She told me, with a quiet conviction, that she had surrendered her life to Jesus. My joy knew no bounds! I felt like the widow who found her lost coin, the shepherd who recovered his lost sheep, and the father who welcomed home his prodigal son. Each of these parables in Luke 15 ends with great rejoicing, not just on earth but in heaven itself.

It is a humbling and awe - inspiring thought that the angels of God rejoice over one sinner who repents. Imagine the music and celebration in heaven when even one heart turns back to God! It reminds me that no effort to share God's love is ever wasted, and that our prayers for others are always heard. Sometimes, we may not see the fruit right away, but God is always at work, quietly and powerfully.

So, let us never give up praying for those who seem far from faith. Let us keep sowing seeds of kindness, truth, and love, trusting that God will bring the growth in His perfect time. And when the lost are found, let us join the angels in rejoicing, for there is no greater miracle than a soul returning home.

All glory be to God!

25

Parable of the Sower

One of the parables that has always fascinated me is the Parable of the Sower, found in Matthew 13. Jesus tells the story of a farmer who goes out to sow seeds. Some seeds fall along the path, some on rocky ground, some among thorns, and some on good soil. The fate of each seed depends entirely on where it lands. As I reflect on this parable at the age of 76, I see more clearly than ever how true it is in both the world around me and in my own heart.

The first kind of soil is the path, where the seeds are quickly eaten by birds. Jesus explains that this represents those who hear the word but do not understand it; the evil one snatches away what was sown in their hearts. I have seen this happen, even in my own family. Sometimes, people hear the message of God's love, but it barely registers before it is gone, drowned out by the noise and distractions of life.

The second kind is the rocky ground. Here, the seeds sprout quickly but wither just as fast because they have no root. These are the people who receive the word with joy but fall away when trouble or persecution comes. I remember times in my own life when I was enthusiastic about my faith, but when difficulties arose, I struggled to hold on. It is easy to be faithful when life is smooth, but real faith is tested in the storms.

The third kind is the soil among thorns. The seeds grow, but the thorns choke them, and they bear no fruit. Jesus says these thorns are the worries of life and the deceitfulness of wealth. How true this is! It is so easy to let anxieties, ambitions, or even daily routines crowd out what matters most. I have learned, sometimes the hard way, that unless we intentionally guard our hearts, the thorns will take over.

But then there is the good soil. Here, the seeds take root, grow, and produce a harvest, multiplied many times over. This is the heart that hears the word, understands it, and puts it into practice. I pray every day that our hearts would be good soil, open and receptive to God's word, willing to let it shape our thoughts, actions, and relationships.

As I tend my little garden, I am reminded that good soil doesn't happen by accident. It takes time, effort, and care to remove stones and weeds, to nourish the ground, and to watch for pests. In the same way, cultivating a fruitful heart requires prayer, reflection, and a willingness to let God do His work in us.

May we all strive to be good soil, ready to receive, grow, and bear fruit for God's kingdom.

All glory be to God!

26

Pigeons Entrapped

Perhaps it is true that those who are deeply rooted in faith and the Word of God are tested "I hate those who pay regard to worthless idols, but I trust in the Lord."

– Psalm 31:6

The other day, as I stood on my balcony, I watched children playing below, their laughter rising up like a song. Suddenly, I heard a frantic shuffling sound. Looking around, I saw a pigeon caught between the pigeon net and the iron framework of the balcony. The poor bird was desperately trying to free itself, but the more it struggled, the more entangled it became. Sometimes its beak was stuck, sometimes its legs, and every attempt to escape only made things worse.

As I watched, my mind wandered to the nets we humans weave around ourselves - nets of lies, deceit, unfaithfulness, covetousness, jealousy, and so many other snares. Like the pigeon, we often find that the harder we try to escape on our own, the more trapped we become. The Psalmist captures this truth in Psalm 9:15: “The nations have sunk in the pit that they made; in the net that they hid, their own foot has been caught.”

The Bible warns us that adultery and idolatry are like traps that can capture us unawares. Adultery, or sexual immorality, creeps in subtly and ensnares the soul. Paul writes in 1 Corinthians 6:9-10, “Do not be deceived: neither the sexually immoral, nor idolaters, nor adulterers, nor men who practice homosexuality, nor thieves, nor the greedy, nor drunkards, nor revilers, nor swindlers will inherit the kingdom of God.” These are not just ancient warnings - they are relevant for us even today.

Idolatry, too, is a snare that reduces us to nothing. It is not just about worshipping golden statues or false gods, as warned in Exodus 23:33 and Deuteronomy 5:6-8. Today’s idols can be wealth, material possessions, success, or even the endless pursuit of validation from others. We may not bow to carved images, but we can become obsessed with celebrities, social media, or the approval of others. All these things can take first place in our lives, pushing God aside.

Unfaithfulness to the true God is not only considered adultery but also idolatry. Isaiah 1:21 describes Jerusalem as a once - faithful city that became a harlot, chasing after other loves. Outward or inward, idolatry is spiritual adultery - breaking our commitment to God in order to love something else. Even in Jesus’ day, people were described as adulterous, despite their religious strictness, because their hearts were far from God.

The Psalmist pleads in Psalm 31:3-6, "Take me out of the net that is hidden for me, for you are my refuge... Into your hand I commit my spirit; you have redeemed me, O Lord, faithful God." Only when we trust in the Lord, turning away from all that entangles us, can we find true freedom. The nets of this world are many, but God's love and faithfulness are greater still.

Let us step back and reflect on what truly matters - cultivating meaningful relationships, showing mercy, kindness, and love, and serving God above all else. May we always trust in the Lord and break free from every snare.

All glory be to God!

27

Beautiful Feet of Those Who Bring Good News

"How beautiful on the mountains are the feet of those who bring good news, who proclaim peace, who bring good tidings, who proclaim salvation, who say to Zion, 'Your God reigns!'"

– Isaiah 52:7

As I reflect on my life's journey at the age of 76, I am often reminded of the countless people who have brought "good news" into my life. Some were family, some friends, and some were strangers who crossed my path for only a moment, yet left a lasting impression. The Bible says their feet are beautiful - not because of their appearance, but because of the message and hope they carry.

I remember, as a young woman, the first time I heard the gospel in a way that touched my heart. It wasn't a grand sermon or a dramatic event, but a gentle conversation with a neighbor who lived her faith quietly and consistently. She listened to my worries, shared her own struggles, and spoke of the peace she found in Jesus. Her words were simple, but they brought light to my life during a dark season. To me, her feet were indeed beautiful, for they brought me hope and the promise of God's love.

Over the years, I have tried to follow her example, sharing the good news in whatever way I could - sometimes through words, sometimes through a kind deed, a letter, or a prayer. I have learned that bringing good news doesn't always mean preaching from a pulpit. Often, it means simply being present, offering a listening ear, or encouraging someone who is weary. God uses our ordinary steps to accomplish extraordinary things.

I think of missionaries and pastors, but also of teachers, nurses, neighbors, and friends who have carried the message of peace and salvation into places of need. Each one, in their own way, has walked a path that made a difference in someone's life. Their journeys may have been long or short, easy or hard, but their willingness to go, to speak, and to serve is what makes their feet beautiful in God's eyes.

As I look at my own feet - now a bit slower, perhaps, but still willing - I pray that God will continue to use me to bring good news, even in small ways. Whether it is a smile, a word of encouragement, or a prayer whispered in faith, I want my steps to be guided by His love.

May we all remember that we are called to be messengers of hope and peace. Let us walk boldly and joyfully, knowing that every step taken in love and obedience is precious to God.

All glory be to God!

28

My Rainy Day Refuge

"You who live in the shelter of the Most High, who abide in the shadow of the Almighty, will say to the Lord, 'My refuge and my fortress; my God, in whom I trust.'"

– Psalm 91:1

The other day, I stepped out of the house to fetch some essentials, not expecting anything unusual. But all of a sudden, the sky darkened and it began to pour. I hadn't thought to bring my umbrella, so I hurried to take shelter under the roof of a closed shop nearby. As I stood there, watching the rain wash the streets, I saw people all around me running for cover. Some ducked under the eaves of houses, others crowded beneath the awnings of shops, and a few simply walked on, unfazed, protected by sturdy umbrellas.

Watching them, I was struck by how much this scene mirrors our spiritual lives. Those with umbrellas walked calmly through the downpour, while the rest of us scrambled for shelter. In that moment, the words of Psalm 91:1 came to mind: *"You who live in the shelter of the Most High… will say to the Lord, 'My refuge and my fortress; my God, in whom I trust."* How true it is! When the heavy drops of distress pour down on us, when waves of grief threaten to overwhelm, when the boat of our life feels as if it might capsize in the storm - there, we find the presence of God, covering us like a protective wing.

I thought of the image Jesus used, like a mother hen stretching out her wings to shield her chicks from the elements. God's covering is just like that - gentle, yet strong; always present, even when storms rage around us.

The Bible is full of such promises. Proverbs 18:10 assures us, *"The name of the Lord is a strong tower; the righteous run into it and are safe."* King David, too, cried out for God's shelter in Psalm 61: *"Hear my cry, O God… Lead me to the rock that is higher than I, for you are my refuge, a strong tower against the enemy."* Again, in Psalm 59, he pleads, *"Deliver me from my enemies, O my God… Protect me from those who rise up against me."*

Time and again, scripture reminds us that God is our keeper, our shade at our right hand (Psalm 121:5), our refuge and strength, a very present help in trouble (Psalm 46:1-3). Even when the earth shakes and the seas roar, we need not fear, for we are safe under His umbrella of protection.

So let us not be anxious when the storms of life come. Instead, let us be drenched in the shower of His assurances and calm ourselves under His divine umbrella. For in every season, God is our shelter, our shade, and our shield. *All glory be to God!*

29

Lean Not on Your Own Understanding

Perhaps it is true that those who are deeply rooted in faith and the Word of God are tested

> *"Trust in the Lord with all your heart, and do not rely on your own understanding. In all your ways acknowledge Him, and He will make straight your paths."*
>
> *– Proverbs 3:5-6*

Yesterday, as I stood on my balcony, I watched a troupe of street acrobats - "dombarata" - performing their daring feats for a small crowd. People from the neighborhood had gathered, laughter and applause filling the air. Suddenly, the mood shifted. The balcony wall of the neighboring house, crowded with onlookers, gave way with a terrible crash. In an instant, people were thrown from their perch. News soon spread that many had sustained injuries - some minor, some grievous - and, heartbreakingly, a couple of people even lost their lives to heart attacks brought on by the shock.

As I looked at the accident site, my heart was heavy. I found myself thinking of the words from Proverbs 3:5-8: *"Trust in the Lord with all your heart, and do not rely on your own insight. In all your ways acknowledge Him, and He will make straight your paths. Do not be wise in your own eyes; fear the Lord and turn away from evil. It will be healing for your flesh and refreshment to your body."* How relevant these words are, even today!

The tragedy, I later learned, was the result of a poorly built balcony. The builder had not used the proper proportions of cement, sand, and bricks. It might have looked sturdy on the outside, but when the pressure mounted, it could not bear the weight. The result was disaster. How often, I thought, do we build our own lives in a similar way - relying on our own wisdom, cutting corners, and leaving God out of our plans?

Life, too, can feel unstable. When sickness batters us, when waves of disappointment and sorrow threaten to overwhelm, it is easy to lose heart. We may feel as if we are tossed into a sea of despair, searching for something solid to hold onto. The truth is, when we lean too much on our own understanding and keep God out of our decisions, we are building on shaky ground.

The Bible is filled with stories of those who trusted God's plan above their own: Abraham setting out for an unknown land, Daniel standing firm in Babylon, Esther risking her life to save her people, Mary accepting God's call despite the risk to her reputation, Peter and Paul obeying God to the end. Their strength came not from their own wisdom, but from a deep reliance on God.

We are called to do the same - to set aside our pride, our plans, and our limited understanding, and to follow the path God has chosen for us. As Jeremiah 29:11 reminds us, God's plans are to prosper us and not to harm us, to give us hope and a future. Even when we cannot see the full picture, His ways are higher and wiser than ours.

Let us pray for the humility and faith to trust God in every circumstance, to become His co - workers in building lives and communities that stand strong - not on our own wisdom, but on His unfailing guidance.

All glory be to God!

30

God's Promise of Restoration

> *"I will repay you for the years that the swarming locust has eaten..."*
>
> *– Joel 2:25*

At 76, I've seen a fair bit of life - Its joys, its losses, and its lessons. One verse that has always given me hope, especially in my later years, is Joel 2:25.

The prophet Joel spoke to a people who had experienced devastation - fields stripped bare by locusts, livelihoods lost, and hope nearly extinguished. Yet, in the midst of judgment and sorrow, God's voice breaks through with a promise: "I will repay you for the years the locusts have eaten."

Human nature, from the very beginning, has been prone to rebellion and wandering away from God. Joel describes how Israel's disobedience brought about the invasion of Assyria and Babylon - a punishment for turning away from the Lord. But

God's anger is not forever. He is abounding in love and mercy, always ready to embrace those who turn back to Him with genuine repentance. Joel 2:16-27 is a beautiful picture of God's willingness to restore, to forgive, and to bless again.

As I meditate on Joel 2:25, I realize that I, too, have sinned many times, especially by disobeying His commandments. Jesus taught that unchecked desire is the root of many troubles. While there is nothing wrong with expecting a fair interest on loans or bank deposits - after all, even in Matthew 25:27 and Luke 19:23, this principle is acknowledged. However, the Old Testament cautions us about greed.

Looking back, I fell prey to the lure of a greedy, unscrupulous co - operative society that dangled the promise of high interest rates before me. At my age, every rupee counts, and the idea of my hard—earned savings multiplying a little faster was tempting—perhaps too tempting. Like a bird drawn to scattered grains, I didn't see the net being laid out for me. I trusted them, believing their words, their brochures, their reassurances.

But all that glitters is not gold. The society, which once seemed so reliable, is now nothing more than a name in old documents. It has collapsed, vanished into thin air, taking with it the hopes of many people like me. The legal battle that follows is slow and exhausting - it drags on endlessly, with no clear end in sight. Each time I hear about another court date, another delay, I feel a pang of helplessness. The money I had set aside for my twilight years, for my family, for emergencies, is locked away in uncertainty.

It's not just the financial loss, though that is painful enough. It's the feeling of being deceived, of having my trust betrayed. After a lifetime of working honestly, to have my savings snatched away by greed and dishonesty is a hard pill to swallow.

Yet, even here, I find hope in God's promise of restoration. Joel's words were first for Israel, but I believe they are for all who trust in God's mercy. The Bible is full of stories where God restores what was lost. When David's family and possessions were stolen by the Amalekites, God enabled him to recover everything (1 Samuel 30:18-20). Psalm 128:1-2 assures us that we will eat the fruit of our labor and be happy. Isaiah 65:21 promises that we will enjoy the work of our hands.

Even with all the frustration and heartache I've described, I find myself anchored by a deep certainty in God's promise of restoration. Joel 2:25 is not just a verse I recite in passing—it is a lifeline that I cling to, especially in times like these. The Lord has pledged to "restore the years that the locusts have eaten," and I believe this assurance stands firm, even when circumstances seem hopeless.

God's restoration isn't always about receiving back exactly what was lost, or having every wrong made right in the way we expect. Sometimes, it is a transformation - a renewal of hope, a strengthening of faith, and the blessing of peace that surpasses understanding. The Bible shows us, time and again, that God delights in turning our seasons of loss into seasons of abundance, and our shame into praise.

So, if you too are grieving lost years or opportunities, take heart. God is still in the business of restoration. He can redeem the locust years and bring joy out of sorrow.

All glory be to Jesus!

31

Discovering Purpose After Loss

In the maze of life, as I wander,
I find myself coming from afar and going nowhere,
I want to read my life, but find no rhythm,
I still go far and far only to find a restless anthem.

– Nirmala Roop Singh

These words, scribbled in a moment of reflection, capture the ache and longing I have often felt in my heart. Now, at 76, as I look back on the long road I have traveled, I sometimes feel a pang of regret for the years that seem to have slipped away without great accomplishment. Much of my life has been spent in the ordinary routines of family and work, and there are moments when I wonder if I have wasted the gifts and opportunities God gave me.

Yet, alongside this regret, I feel a deep sense of satisfaction. I know I have been a blessing to my family, even if my own dreams - especially my love for literature - had to take a back seat. My parents had wanted me to pursue science, and though my heart longed for literature, I followed their wishes. I would steal moments in the library, immersing myself in Kannada and English books, feeding my soul with stories and poetry. But as life moved on, a government job, marriage, children, and the building of a new home took priority.

Illness and loss visited our home often. My husband endured open heart surgery, angioplasties, and cataracts. I faced my own share of health struggles: cataract surgeries, a pacemaker, knee replacement, thrombectomy, angioplasty, and even a mastectomy. Each trial demanded time, energy, and faith. And then, the greatest loss - my husband's passing - left me feeling utterly alone in the maze of life.

But God, in His faithfulness, never let go of my hand. Even when I felt I had lost so much - time, health, dreams - He was quietly working to restore what the "locusts" had eaten. Joel 2:25 became a lifeline for me: "I will repay you for the years that the swarming locust has eaten, the hopper, the destroyer, and the cutter, my great army, which I sent against you." I clung to this promise, believing that God's barns of blessing are never empty.

Now, in this quieter season, I find myself returning to my first love - literature. I have written two books, one in English and one in Kannada, recounting my encounters with God's grace and mercy. In these pages, I see how God truly restores what was lost. He gives back not just time, but joy, purpose, and hope.

I am convinced that God will continue to restore all that I have lost - my time, my relationships, my peace. He is a faithful, promise - keeping God. May He do for you what He has done for me: restore your lost years and fill your life with new songs of gratitude.

All glory be to God!

32

Our Good Shepherd Is Our Judge Too

"When the Son of Man comes in his glory, and all the angels with him, then he will sit on the throne of his glory. All the nations will be gathered before him, and he will separate people one from another as a shepherd separates the sheep from the goats."

– Matthew 25:31-32

The other day, as I was cleaning grains in my kitchen, I noticed some black worms in the bottle where I stored green gram dal. Without hesitation, I emptied the bottle into a sieve and shook it vigorously. Soon, all the worms fell away, leaving behind only the clean, uncontaminated grains. As I watched the separation, my mind turned to the words of Jesus in Matthew 25, where He speaks of the final judgment.

Jesus, our Good Shepherd, is also our Judge. He spoke to His disciples about the day when He will return in glory, surrounded by angels, and all nations will be gathered before Him. On that day, He will separate people as a shepherd separates sheep from goats. The sheep - those who have shown love, mercy, and faithfulness - will be welcomed into eternal life. The goats - those who ignored the needs of others and lived for themselves - will go away into eternal punishment.

This teaching is sobering. It reminds me that our everyday actions and words matter deeply. Just as I sifted the grains, keeping only the good and pure, so too will Jesus examine our lives. He will see not just what we did outwardly, but the motives of our hearts. It is a call to be diligent, to live with integrity, and to care for our neighbors, for in serving others, we serve Christ Himself.

Jesus warns us to be prepared, to discern truth from falsehood, and to beware of those who would lead us astray. He cautions us against careless words and empty deeds. In Matthew 12:36-37, He says, "I tell you, on the day of judgment, you will have to give an account for every careless word you utter; for by your words you will be justified, and by your words you will be condemned." Our words and actions are like seeds sown in the field of life; one day, the harvest will be gathered and sorted.

Yet, there is also hope and promise. Jesus assures His faithful followers that they will share in His Kingdom. In Matthew 19:28-29 and Luke 22:28-30, He promises that those who have stood by Him, who have sacrificed for His sake, will receive a hundredfold and inherit eternal life. Paul echoes this in Romans 2:6-8, reminding us that God will repay each person according to what they have done - persistent goodness will be rewarded with eternal life.

As I reflect on these truths, I am reminded to live each day with purpose and humility, trusting in Jesus not only as my Shepherd but also as my righteous Judge. May we be found among the sheep, faithful and true, ready to enter into the joy of our Master.

All glory be to God!

33

Our Debts, Paid in Full

> *"Jesus has rescued us from the power of darkness and transferred us into the kingdom of his beloved Son, in whom we have redemption, the forgiveness of sins."*
>
> *– Colossians 1:13-14*

Throughout my life, I have seen how debt can weigh a person down. Whether it's a loan from a neighbor or a sum owed to the bank, the burden of repayment is never far from our minds. The Old Testament tells us of many who struggled under such burdens. I am reminded of the widow in 2 Kings 4:2-7, who cried out to the prophet Elisha when her husband's death left her in desperate debt. By God's mercy, Elisha helped her find a way out, multiplying her oil so she could pay what she owed and live free.

But there is a far greater debt that every one of us carries - the debt of sin. No amount of money, power, or good deeds can ever pay it off. Romans 6:23 tells us plainly, "The wages of sin is death, but the gift of God is eternal life in Christ Jesus our Lord." Sin entered the world so subtly through Adam and Eve, and since then, humanity has been crushed under its weight. We are, as Paul says, "slaves to sin," desperately in need of someone to rescue us.

The good news is that Jesus came to do just that. Galatians 5:1 proclaims, "For freedom Christ has set us free. Stand firm, therefore, and do not submit again to a yoke of slavery." In John 8:34-36, Jesus Himself says, "Very truly, I tell you, everyone who commits sin is a slave to sin… so if the Son makes you free, you will be free indeed." Jesus, the Son of God, became our mediator, standing in the gap between us and a holy God.

Scripture is full of examples of people who stood in the gap for others - Abraham interceding for Sodom, Moses pleading for Israel, Paul praying for his people, Stephen forgiving his executioners. But none compare to Jesus, who from the cross prayed, *"Father, forgive them, for they do not know what they are doing"* (Luke 23:34). Hebrews 7:25 assures us that Jesus "always lives to intercede" for us.

Jesus paid our debt in full - He took on Himself the punishment we deserved, liberating us from the bondage of sin, a debt He never owed. The love, kindness, and mercy shown by our Savior are beyond compare. All He asks in return is that we acknowledge Him as our Lord and Savior, confessing with our hearts and lives that He is the Son of God, raised from the dead for our salvation.

Paul gently reminds us, *"Owe no one anything, except to love one another"* (Romans 13:8). Our only remaining "debt" is to love, for in loving, we fulfill God's law.

Let us rejoice in the freedom Christ has won for us, living as children of God, grateful and free.

All glory be to God!

34

The Barren Fig Tree

"When he saw a fig tree by the road, he went up to it but found nothing on it except leaves. Then he said to it, 'May you never bear fruit again!' Immediately the tree withered."

– Matthew 21:19

For many years, I found the story of Jesus cursing the fig tree in Matthew 21:18-22 quite puzzling. At first glance, it seemed unfair - after all, it wasn't even the season for figs! Why would Jesus curse a tree for not bearing fruit out of season? But as I pondered and prayed over this passage, I began to see its deeper meaning, both for the people of Jesus' day and for us today.

Fig trees in the Bible are symbols of abundance, blessing, and spiritual fruitfulness. They also represent the people of God, especially Jerusalem. In the Old Testament, prophets like Jeremiah used the fig tree to symbolize God's call to repentance and the consequences of spiritual barrenness (see Jeremiah 19:1-11).

When Jesus approached the fig tree, it was full of leaves, giving the impression of fruitfulness. But on closer inspection, there was no fruit at all - only empty show.

This is the heart of the lesson. Jesus was not angry with the tree itself, but with what it represented: the danger of outward appearances without inward reality. The tree looked healthy, but it was barren. In the same way, Jesus saw many religious leaders and followers in His time who had all the signs of faith - knowledge of Scripture, public prayers, strict observance of rituals - but lacked the true fruit of love, obedience, and faithfulness.

In Matthew 23, Jesus rebukes the Pharisees and scribes for their hypocrisy. They looked holy on the outside but were empty within. He warns us, too, not to settle for a faith that is all leaves and no fruit. True discipleship is not about looking good or being admired by others; it is about bearing the fruit of the Spirit - love, joy, peace, patience, kindness, goodness, faithfulness, gentleness, and self - control.

Jesus expects His followers to bear fruit in every season - not just when it is convenient or easy. He warns against hypocrisy and calls us to authentic living. Our actions must match our beliefs. We are called to live out our faith in practical ways, showing kindness, mercy, and generosity, even when no one is watching.

The story of the barren fig tree is a warning, but also an invitation. Jesus invites us to examine our lives, to repent of empty religion, and to seek a faith that is alive and fruitful. May we not be found with only leaves, but with the abundant fruit that brings glory to God and blessing to others.

May our Lord help us to live worthy of His calling and to bear much fruit in the vineyard of His kingdom.

All glory be to God!

35

Membership in God's Kingdom

When we think about joining an exclusive club or a prestigious academy, we know there are always rules and requirements. We meticulously follow each step, pay hefty membership fees, and sometimes even adhere to strict dress codes, all to secure a place among the chosen few. Even citizenship in a country demands loyalty, commitment, and often a substantial financial investment.

But there is one kingdom, ancient and everlasting, whose membership is unlike any other. The Kingdom of God stands apart from all earthly organizations. Its gates are open to all, and the cost of entry is not measured in money or merit. In fact, the price has already been paid - by someone infinitely rich in mercy, kindness, and love. The sign above the entrance reads boldly: "Entry by Grace Alone."

What a marvel this is! While earthly citizenships require us to earn our place, the Kingdom of God welcomes us freely. The only requirement is that we come washed in the blood of Jesus, clothed in the white garments of righteousness, with the image of Christ engraved on our hearts. Our passport is not a document, but a heart surrendered to Jesus and a life committed to obeying Him.

But what is grace, and how do we receive it? Grace is the foundation of our Christian faith. It is God's undeserved favor, freely given and never earned. Grace and faith are two sides of the same coin - inseparable and essential. Grace cannot be achieved by good works or personal merit; it is a gift, flowing from the very character of God. As Paul writes in Romans 3:23-24, *"All have sinned and fall short of the glory of God; they are now justified by His grace as a gift, through the redemption that is in Christ Jesus."*

We see the theme of grace running through both the Old and New Testaments. Numbers 6:24-26 offers the blessing, *"The Lord bless you and keep you… The Lord make His face shine upon you and be gracious to you."* Psalm 103:8 reminds us, "The Lord is merciful and gracious, slow to anger and abounding in steadfast love." Isaiah 30:18 assures us, *"The Lord waits to be gracious to you… for the Lord is a God of justice; blessed are all those who wait for Him."*

In the New Testament, grace is embodied in Jesus, "full of grace and truth" (John 1:14). Paul reminds us in Ephesians 2:8-9, *"For by grace you have been saved through faith, and this is not your own doing; it is the gift of God, not the result of works, so that no one may boast."* Grace is the undercurrent of our lives, sustaining us through every trial and triumph.

We cannot boast of our place in God's Kingdom. It is not our achievement, but His gift. All He asks is that we come humbly, receive His grace, and live in gratitude and obedience. The doors are open, the fee is paid, and the invitation is for everyone.

All glory be to God!

36

The Second Key to Kingdom Entry

We understand that the worlds were prepared by the word of God, so that what is seen was made from things that are not visible."

– Hebrews 11:1-3

After reflecting on the marvelous truth that entry into God's Kingdom is by grace alone, we now come to the second great "membership rule": faith. While grace is God's free gift to us, faith is our response - our hand reaching out to receive all He offers.

Faith, as the writer of Hebrews tells us, is the assurance of things hoped for and the conviction of things not seen. It is trusting in God's character and promises, even when we cannot see the outcome. Hebrews 11, often called the "Hall of Faith," gives us a glorious list of men and women who lived by faith: Abel, Enoch,

Noah, Abraham, Sarah, Isaac, Jacob, Joseph, Moses, Joshua, Rahab, Gideon, Barak, Samson, Jephthah, David, Samuel, Daniel, Shadrach, Meshach, Abednego, and many others. Their lives were marked by trust in God's word, even when it seemed impossible.

Abraham's faith was counted to him as righteousness (Genesis 15:6). James echoes this, calling Abraham a "friend of God" because of his unwavering belief (James 2:23). Faith is not just believing in God - it is believing God. It is staking our lives on His promises, even when the evidence is not yet visible. The beginning of faith is believing that God is who He says He is; the end of faith is trusting that He will do what He has promised.

Many of the heroes of faith never saw the full fruit of their trust while on earth. Yet, they continued to believe, knowing that God is always faithful. Hebrews 11:6 reminds us, *"Without faith it is impossible to please God, for whoever would approach Him must believe that He exists and that He rewards those who seek Him."* Noah built an ark before a single drop of rain fell; Abraham set out for a land he had never seen; Moses led a people through the wilderness, trusting in God's provision.

Faith is the cornerstone of discipleship. The righteous live by faith, not by sight. Even when God seems slow to act, the faithful continue to trust, obey, and remain loyal. Faith is the bridge that connects us to God's grace and mercy. My husband once wrote, "Mercy is getting what we do not deserve; grace is not getting what we do deserve." When we were sinners, Jesus gathered us to Himself by His mercy and bore the penalty we deserved by His grace.

May we, too, be counted among the faithful - those who trust God's promises, obey His word, and walk by faith, not by sight. Let us hold fast to the assurance that, through faith, we belong to the Kingdom of God.

All glory be to God!

37

The Unwed Couple

As we celebrate Christmas, we commemorate the birth of Jesus Christ, who descended to Earth to give mankind a rebirth. During this time, we focus on Jesus as an infant. The word "infant" evokes a sense of weakness, helplessness, and frailty, along with hope, strength, and stability. It is a source of encouragement and enlightenment for parents and loved ones.

An infant cannot survive on its own. It needs help and sustenance, which in most cases comes from the mother. In unfortunate circumstances where the mother is absent, support is provided by kind - hearted, generous individuals who stand by and extend their help.

Though Jesus was omnipotent, when presented to us as an infant, he was frail and needed his mother Mary's support. Imagining Mary as a poor mother, struggling to keep her baby warm by swaddling him with clothes to protect from the cold breeze in the makeshift manger, one can envision her plight in managing the cold winter season of Bethlehem in the Middle East.

Although the Christ child, being the Son of God, was entitled to all kinds of comfort, he was made to undergo humiliation, suffering, and shame from the beginning of his earthly life, with mother Mary as a witness.

One day, news reached me about an unmarried woman in our neighbourhood who had delivered a baby. As neighbours reacted with pity and sympathy, my mind wandered to Mary, mother of Jesus, and how she might have felt upon learning she would become a mother without being married.

Contemplating Mary's experiences, I find many things conspicuously woven around her that went unnoticed and didn't find a place in the Bible. The first thing that came to mind was that she was to be an unwed mother. We know the stigma attached to unwed mothers in our society, and the contemporary society in which Mary lived was no exception.

The society that dragged a woman caught in adultery into public, shaming her, didn't feel it "appropriate" to bring the man too to justice, despite being a partner in the same sin. In such a scenario, Mary's plight when discovered with child must have been difficult. Although an angel convinced Joseph that the child was conceived by the Holy Spirit, convincing society would have been challenging.

Mary lived among her family and friends daily. Were her parents, relatives, and friends okay with her conceiving out of wedlock?

They might have slandered and shamed her, unaware of the divine nature of her pregnancy.

Yet, we see Mary as an obedient girl, willing to surrender herself to God's will, braving all odds and slander from contemporary society at the cost of her own character and reputation. Her response to the angel's greeting demonstrates her faith: "Here I am, the servant of the Lord; let it be with me according to your word" (Luke 1:38).

Joseph, Mary's fiancé, also showed remarkable obedience to God. When he learned of Mary's pregnancy, he had the right to divorce her according to Jewish culture. However, he chose to obey God's message delivered through an angel. Joseph's actions reveal admirable qualities such as principles, discretion, sensitivity to the situation, responsiveness to God, and self - discipline.

Both Mary and Joseph serve as perfect examples of obedience to God, prioritizing truth and divine will over societal approval. They can be considered heroes of great faith alongside other biblical figures like Daniel, Shadrach, Meshach, Abednego, Paul, Peter, and other disciples of Jesus.

May God bless the exposition of His words and bless us all.

All glory be to God!

Acknowledgements

As I come to the end of these reflections, I want to pause and say a heartfelt thank you to all those who have stood by me during these trying times. Truly, I am blessed with a wonderful circle of family and friends who have upheld me in prayer, encouraged me with their words, and sometimes even just listened to me.

A very special thank you goes to my dear daughter, Christabel. She's been my rock - always there to inspire me, even when she's juggling a hundred things of her own. Of course, we've had our share of mother - daughter squabbles over how long this book has taken to see the light of day. But through it all, her love and persistence have been a true blessing.

I must also thank Reverend Ravi Sebastian, whose wise counsel and prayers have lifted my spirits more than once. His faith in God's restoration has helped me keep my own faith strong, even on the days when I felt like giving up.

My gratitude also goes to Smt. Harshitha and Smt. Tanuja Honey, who helped me with the English and Kannada transcriptions. And to everyone who prayed for me - your prayers have been the quiet strength behind my hope.

Thank you, each and every one of you, for walking this road with me. My dearest hope for this book is that it will bring comfort and encouragement to anyone who finds themselves in seasons of loss or waiting. If you, too, have faced setbacks, disappointments, or moments when you wondered if God's promises still hold true, may these pages remind you that you are not alone.

May you find renewed faith, a little laughter, and the certainty that God's restoration is always at work, sometimes in ways we least expect.

With love and gratitude,

Nirmala Roop Singh